Inside-out

Acknowledgement

With thanks to students, friends and family who helped.

Inside-out

Ruth Gravelle

EGON PUBLISHERS LIMITED
Royston Road
Baldock, Herts SG7 6NW

ISBN 1 904160 85 9

Printed by Streets Printers
Royston Road, Baldock, Hertfordshire SG7 6NW, England

Published by
Egon Publishers Limited
Royston Road, Baldock, Hertfordshire SG7 6NW, England

Introduction

My first idea was to produce a book about dyslexia using pictures and very few words. However, it has ended up with hundreds of words because I couldn't say as much as I wanted to with the pictures alone.

The book aims to:

- describe dyslexia through pictures and words
- show how it can feel to experience dyslexia
- help people to understand dyslexia, recognise their potential and develop skills and strategies to cope.

I am a specialist dyslexia teacher and work mainly with teenage and adult students. I am dyslexic myself as are my son and several other relatives. I hardly ever read for pleasure and can't remember names of many films or the people who act in them. I don't need to wear glasses, but do carry a spellchecker in my handbag!

I found school extremely difficult and left with only two GCSEs. My dyslexia was officially recognised at the age of twenty-seven. It was a huge relief when the Educational Psychologist said "Yes, you are dyslexic." I felt this gave me permission to have the difficulties that I have. Since then, I have been finding out more about dyslexia.

The pictures that I have drawn in this book come from my experiences as a dyslexic person and through what I have learned by meeting and working with other dyslexic people and their families. It seems likely that you will identify with several pictures in this book if you are dyslexic.

What is dyslexia?

Dyslexia can be understood as a kind of 'mechanical problem' where weaknesses in our working memories can make it difficult for us to...

It can sometimes be as challenging and frustrating for dyslexic people to read, write and follow conversation as it may have been for you to decipher the text within this picture.

Dyslexia may be 'mechanical' but it feels personal

Today's society expects us all to read, write and remember things.

We grow up expecting these things of ourselves.

When dyslexia is not recognised or appropriately supported it can be an uncomfortable experience.

Who is likely to be dyslexic?

Dyslexia is usually an hereditary condition. So if you are dyslexic it's likely that other family members such as a parent, grandparent, brother, sister or cousin will have similar difficulties.

Dyslexia and intelligence

It doesn't make any difference what your intellectual ability is;
people of high, average and lower intelligence can show signs of dyslexia.

What percentage of the population is dyslexic?

The British Dyslexia Association suggests that about 10% of children are dyslexic; other research studies have indicated higher and lower figures.

Are there more dyslexic males than females?

Most research indicates that there are more male than female dyslexics.

Are some people are more dyslexic than others?

Yes. The severity of dyslexia varies from person to person. No two cases of dyslexia are exactly the same.

Will dyslexia go away?

No. We are born with dyslexia and we'll still be dyslexic when we die. But, that's all right because there's nothing wrong with being dyslexic.

Spoonerisms

Words, letters and sounds can sometimes come out in

the wrong order when we are reading, writing and talking.

The Reverend Spooner (1844-1930) is said to have

frequently misplaced the sounds in words as he spoke.

Instead of saying "In the name of the Father," he may have said $\longrightarrow$

These kinds of slips are now known as spoonerisms.

The Reverend Spooner is thought to have been dyslexic.

The writing experience

David cannot get his thoughts onto the page in the right order

"... and I can't spell properly."

Right one day and wrong the next

Tony worked very hard and learned to spell all the words for his test. The following day he wrote a story and misspelled them all. The reason this happened was because he had to focus on many other tasks at the same time. These included thinking about what to write, remembering to use a capital letter and full stop and getting the sentences in the right order. The story writing task placed too many demands on his working memory.

If like Tony you are dyslexic, remember you are not lazy or stupid.
Your dyslexia means you are a 'quick forgetter' not a 'slow learner.'

Tony felt disappointed and angry when his work had been marked and he flushed it down the lavatory.

Difficulty in retrieving words

... and finding the collective name for things!

Fiona can see the apple, banana, tangerine, orange and grapes in her mind's eye and she can remember their names, but she can't find the word "f...."

Mary hid her reading problem

From the age of seven Mary recognised that the books were too difficult
for her but she couldn't tell anybody. She used to pretend that she was
reading, turning the pages over at the same rate as everyone else.
Mary used a lot of energy 'hiding' her difficulty with reading.

When the teacher asked Mary what her book was about, she had no idea.

The reading experience

Reading aloud is recalled by many teenagers and adults as one of the most humiliating things that happened to them at school.

If you are still at school and feel uncomfortable about being asked to read out loud, tell your teacher and the school SENCO (Special Educational Needs Co-ordinator). If you don't tell them they won't know or be able to help.

Overlays

Olive tried all the colours and felt relieved when she placed the green one on the white paper!

Overlays don't work for everybody, but they worked for Olive and they
might work for you.

John's experience

At school he threw paper aeroplanes, pens and the occasional chair. He refused to read aloud, swore at teachers, punched the wall and slammed the door in a cursing rage when his teacher held up his work and said he'd got it all wrong.

"I couldn't understand the work and was given detention after detention, so in the end I got myself expelled."

John is now 40 years old and married to a teacher. He has a high IQ and considerable dyslexic difficulties.

...and he is studying for a degree in design.

How Ray coped

Ray couldn't experience success at school by writing a good essay, understanding a comprehension passage, reading aloud or finding many words in the dictionary.

He felt unhappy about these things, but soon discovered that when he joked around his classmates laughed and laughed. This 'clowning' behaviour made him feel popular and accepted by the other children. They would dare him do things and he did them. Ray got into a lot of trouble and he was blamed for stopping the other children from learning. He was constantly told to stop messing around and get on with his work.

Things could have been so much easier for everybody in the classroom if Ray's dyslexia had been recognised and supported.

Now Ray is grown up he can see why all this happened.

Who's dyslexic in this family?

The Green-nose family don't believe in dyslexia!

Some families deny the existence of dyslexia or hold the view that there is no point in labelling their child as dyslexic.

In my opinion it's important that dyslexia is recognised and understood by the whole family.

How does Charles feel?

Confusion between left and right

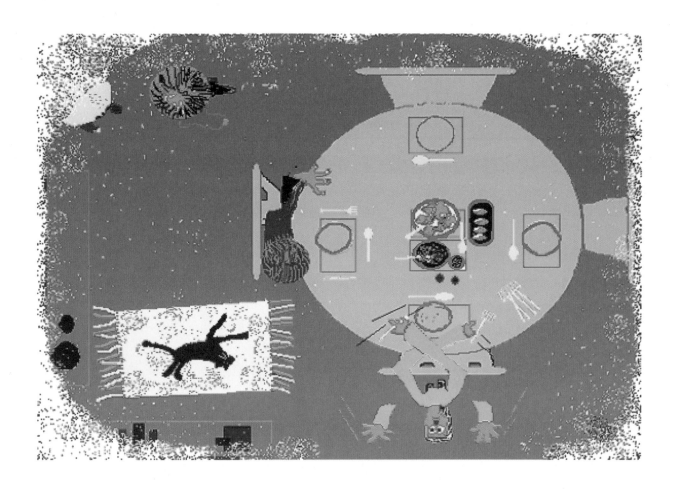

Louise does not know which way round to place the knives and forks.

When you are dyslexic there is every excuse for mistakes when copying from the board.

I remember frequently losing my place when copying at school. I also recall the work being wiped away before I had a chance to write it down. If this happens to you, tell your teacher and ask if you can sit close to the front and face the middle of the board.

Teachers and lecturers can also help by:

- minimising the amount of information that needs to be copied
- keeping sentences short
- using bullet points
- where possible allowing students to have copies of key notes before lectures or lessons.

Using the dictionary

"I can't look up the word if I don't know how to spell it!"

You could try using an **Ace Spelling Dictionary** (see note 1). This is a very different kind of dictionary because you find words from the way they sound. This type of dictionary suits some dyslexic people.

Others find a **spellchecker** or a **speaking spellchecker** faster and easier to use than the dictionary (see note 2).

Another good idea is to buy a small index book and write some of the words in it that you know you spell wrongly.

Whilst it's true that dictionaries, the Yellow Pages and phone books are often frustrating and difficult to use, it can still be a good idea to practise using them. This is because sequencing problems, such as looking for things in alphabetical order, can improve!

A dyslexia friendly filing cabinet!

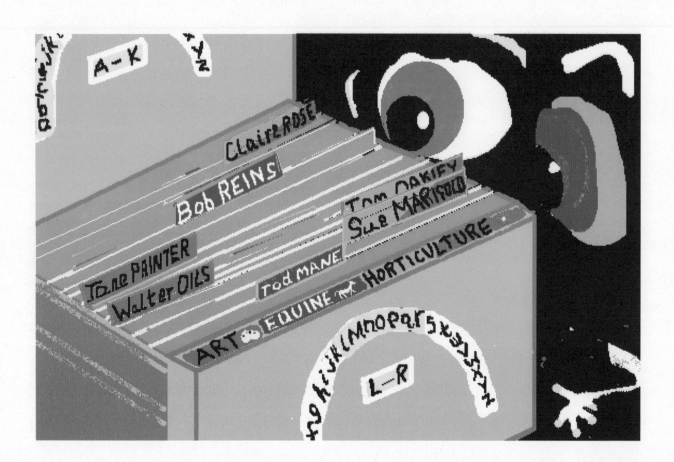

This filing system is easier to use because:

- the letter arc on the front of the drawer shows the alphabet and its sequence

- the student files are colour-coded with picture symbols.

Have you tried mnemonics?

It's good to think of your own mnemonics. The ruder, the better! We remember things best that excite us, disgust us and make us laugh.

Dictation and note taking

Taking dictation or note taking, in other words listening to what somebody is saying and writing down at the same time, can be very difficult when you are dyslexic. This is because by the time you have concentrated on writing the first few words that were said, you have forgotten what the remainder of the sentence was.

Taking dictation is also difficult when you have a slow writing speed. Some dyslexics can find dictation difficult because they have messy handwriting and find it impossible to read their own work afterwards.

Spelling is often worse than usual because there's no time to think about how to spell a word when you are taking down dictation at what feels to you like a supersonic speed.

"I only have time to catch a few words.

When I look at what I have written, it doesn't make any sense."

Use whatever method works for you

If you find dictation or note taking difficult, some of the following strategies may help:

- tape record the lesson or lecture
- if you can type quickly, use a laptop computer or word processor
- take notes using a **mind map** (see note 3)
- ask if you can have lesson notes or photocopy a friend's work
- reduce what you need to write down by using some symbols such as '&' instead of 'and', and .˙. instead of 'therefore' & make up your own abbreviations.

47

Computers

There are a lot of software programmes that can help dyslexic people. You could try using a programme such as **Texthelp Read and Write** on your computer (see note 2). You type the words, and the programme reads them back to you. You can hear your mistakes because the computer voice reads them to you.

The Library

Many dyslexic people have enormous difficulty finding books in the library. Some have a fear of the library. If you have problems like this, I recommend you ask the Librarian for help. Librarians actually like books and they know just where to find them!

Some libraries allow longer book loans for dyslexic people. This is helpful because when you are dyslexic it can take a long time to read.

Paul forgot

Paul likes P.E. It is a lesson where he succeeds. He did not forget to bring his kit to school on purpose.

If you identify with this kind of situation, remember it was not your fault that you forgot. We cannot change the past, but we can do something about our problem with remembering things. I recommend using a timetable or diary. This will do the remembering for you, providing of course that you remember to use it!

Do you often miss appointments?

Many dyslexic people have a poor understanding of time and are often late for appointments.

Understanding the concept of time usually gets easier as we get older and many dyslexic adults are extremely well organised. They do not miss appointments because they have learned strategies to cope.

They:

- write things down
- tape-record them
- set the alarm on their mobile phone.

This can make things much easier.

Sue tried to phone her friend

Sue often dials wrong numbers; she has problems filling in forms, following directions and remembering instructions. Sue felt misunderstood by her teachers and didn't cope well at school. Sue never learned her multiplication tables.

Whilst most of the pictures in this book show younger people, it is important to recognise that there are just as many older people experiencing dyslexia.

Dyslexia and Music

Reading music and understanding rhythm can also be difficult.

This picture came together as I remember middle C as the London Underground symbol, hence the train and perhaps the depth of the underground, which I find scary! The tracks soon collapse, disappear or disintegrate. This is what happens to the music and rhythm when I try to sight read. The treble clef represents the authority figure and there is not enough time to meet its demands.

Don't let this put you off; there are plenty of musicians who do not read music well. If you want to play the piano…then play the piano! There are also many talented dyslexic musicians who learn to read music competently (see further reading).

I am not aware if the condition of 'difficulty with music' has a name. Maybe it could be called 'Dysmusicallia'!

Notes like words, can come and go as they please.

Dyslexia and Maths

Dyslexia may include weaknesses in maths. You might find it difficult or impossible to store the numbers in your head and remember maths symbols such as **+**, **−**, × and **=**. You may have confusion about all the different maths words that can mean the same thing. For example:

+	−
plus	minus
add	subtract
addition	subtraction
the sum of	difference
increase	decrease
more than	less than
total	take away

It could be that you have never learned the multiplication tables, find it difficult to remember how to do long division, fractions or work out percentages. Some dyslexic people can't count to twenty without going wrong.

So, dyslexia may include some maths problems. There are also some non-dyslexic people who only have problems with maths. These people are said to experience dyscalculia.

"I have nowhere to store the numbers in my head
and they disappear whilst I try to do the sum."

Are you good at daydreaming?

You may have used daydreaming as a coping strategy at school in order to avoid work you could not follow. The good news is that the daydreaming will have helped you to develop your imagination which can be used to help you picture and remember information and ideas.

Thinking in pictures

The right side of our brain can be
thought about as dealing mainly with...   ...and the left with...

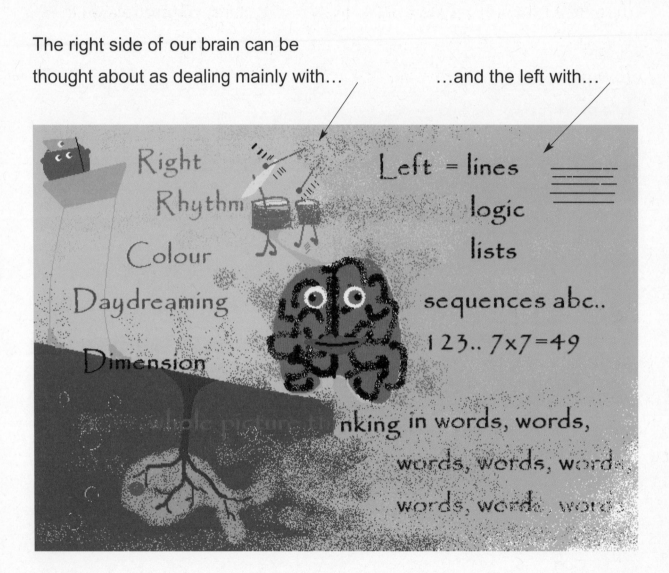

Many dyslexics have above average strengths in visual-spatial cognitive ability, which means an extra ability to think in pictures. This is related to strengths in the right side of the brain and could explain why John shown on page 27 is studying for a degree in design!

The visual strengths that dyslexia can bring are highlighted by the work of the **Arts Dyslexia Trust** (see General notes and Organisations). Dyslexic people often find satisfaction in careers where they can use and develop visual strengths. For instance, many architects

artists

designers

sculptors

musicians

inventors

engineers

photographers

computer workers

and poets...are dyslexic.

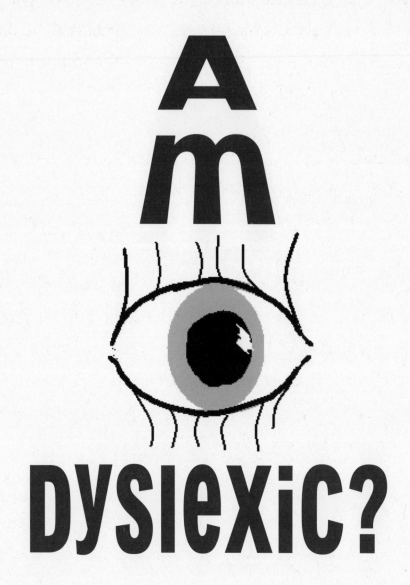

Am I DysIexiC?

If you think you may be dyslexic and feel that it's holding you back, I recommend that you get it diagnosed. You could contact the **Adult Dyslexia Organisation** or the **British Dyslexia Association** for advice (see General notes and Organisations).

If you are a student at school, college or university, a visit to the support unit to discuss your learning needs would be appropriate. It's worth finding out what kind of help is available. You may be eligible for exam provision, such as extra time, a reader and a scribe (see further reading). You may be offered an assessment for dyslexia, individual or group support and equipment loans such as spellcheckers and dictaphones. Higher Education students who are dyslexic may be eligible for the **Disabled Students Allowance** (DSA) (see note 5). The support unit may have a test kit for overlays (mentioned on page 24) or refer you to a specialist optometrist who knows about dyslexia and vision.

YOU are in control of your learning.

Mental energy

Imagine that we each have a bundle of 'invisible' mental energy. How much energy do you use to hide your dyslexia? Does it need to be hidden?

It's okay to be angry and upset about having been misunderstood in the past. Talking about it with somebody who understands can help. You are not stupid and there's nothing wrong with being dyslexic. As dyslexic people we do have weaknesses in our working memory and we may also have strengths in visual-spatial thinking.

More skills and strategies to cope with dyslexic difficulties can be learned and used. The best way to learn is in a multi-sensory way. This means using many senses at the same time. In other words: say it, see it, hear it, feel it, imagine it, laugh about it, sing it… and this will help us to learn.

Find out how you remember things best.

I hope this book has helped.

Write things down, tape-record them and draw them.

P.S.

The Late Professor Meredith described dyslexia as the Unidentified Flying Object of Psychology (see note 4).

Notes

1. **Ace Spelling Dictionary**
   Moseley, D 1986 *Ace Spelling Dictionary*, LDA, ISBN 1 85503 214 7

2. **Spellcheckers**, computer software such as **Texthelp Read and Write**
   and other resources are available from iANSYST Ltd,
   telephone: 0800 018 0045. Web: www.dyslexic.com

3. **Mind maps** were introduced by Tony Buzan during the 1960s. A mind
   map can help you to organise ideas and plan just about anything, for
   example, a holiday, a shopping list or an essay. Mind maps can look just
   how you want them to because they come from the mind of the person
   who draws them. Buzan explains about mind maps and gives examples
   in his book.
   Buzan (1995), **Use Your Head**, BBC Books, ISBN 0 563 37103 X.

4. **P.S. (Post Script)**. This illustration was partly inspired by the words of
   the late Professor Meredith of the University of Leeds who described
   dyslexia as 'The unidentified flying object of psychology'. This was
   referred to by Pumfrey, P and Reason, R 1991, **Specific Learning
   Difficulties (Dyslexia) Challenges and Responses**, Routledge,
   London. ISBN 0 415 06470 8.

5. **Disabled Students Allowance (DSA)** A booklet called 'Bridging the
   Gap' for Higher Education students explains the DSA. Call freephone
   0800 731 9133 for information. Web: www.dfes.gov.uk/studentsupport